STEP INTO SCIENCE

UP, UP & AWAY!

The Science of Flight

BARBARA TAYLOR

★ ★ ★ ★ ★ ★ ★ ★ ★ ★ ★ ★ ★

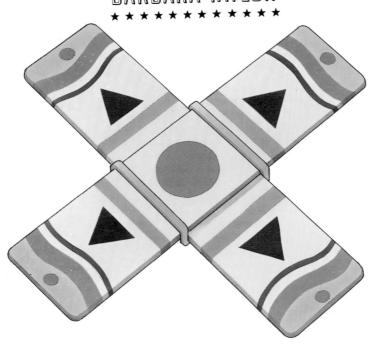

RANDOM HOUSE 🏠 NEW YORK

AIR AND FLIGHT

In this book, you will discover why we need air to survive, how the weather is caused by moving air, and how machines and animals fly through the air.

The book is divided into six different subjects. Watch for the big headings with a circle at each end—like the one at the top of this page. These headings tell you where a new subject starts.

Pages 4–11

Air All Around

Air every day; breathing air; burning; rusting; air in cooking.

Pages 12–15

Warm Air, Cold Air

Hot-air balloons; convection currents.

Pages 16–19

Air Pushes Back

Compressed air; air pressure; siphons; air cushion vehicles.

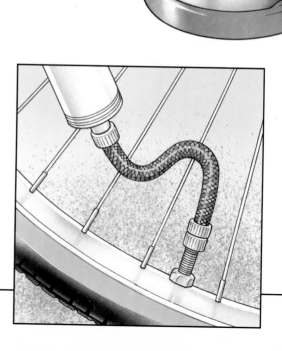

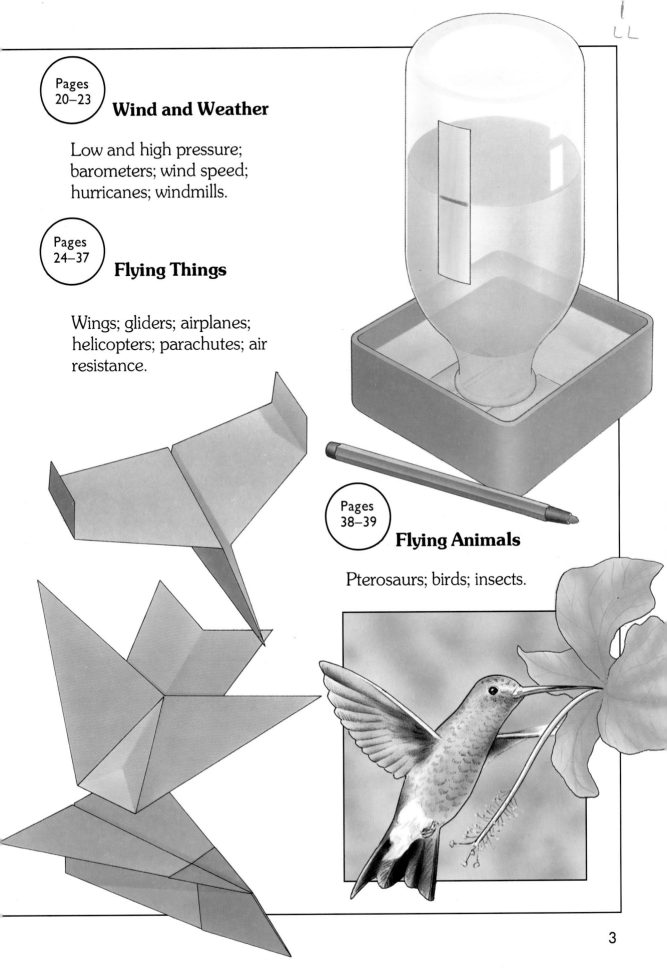

Air is everywhere. It fills the space all around you. It is inside plants and animals, cups and saucepans, bicycle tires and balloons. Soil and water also contain air. Because we cannot see, smell, or taste air, we often forget that it is there. The best way to investigate air is to look at what it does to things around you.

The pictures along the bottom of these two pages will give you some ideas. How many more examples can you think of? Make up a story or write a poem about how air affects your life.

Bubbles of air in a fizzy drink

▶ When air moves from place to place, we call it wind. A windy day is a good time to fly a kite. The force of the wind pushes the kite up into the sky.

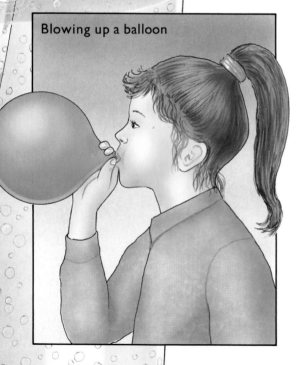
Blowing up a balloon

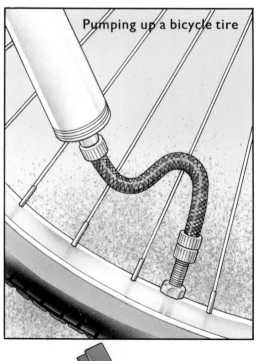
Pumping up a bicycle tire

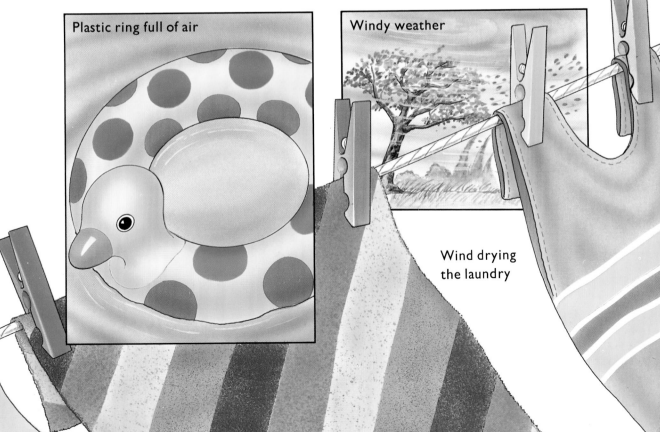

Plastic ring full of air

Windy weather

Wind drying
the laundry

 **Breath Power**

Why do you need air? When you inhale (breathe in), air is sucked into your lungs. In your lungs, one of the gases in the air—called oxygen—passes into your blood. The blood carries oxygen to every part of your body. You need oxygen to release the energy stored in your food. Without oxygen, you could not survive. All plants and animals need the oxygen in the air to stay alive.

Count how many times you inhale during one minute. Then run in place or up and down stairs for one minute and count again. Repeat the same test after standing still for five minutes or after swimming or riding your bike. Compare all your results.

You can also feel your pulse before and after exercising. To do this, place a finger on the side of your neck or on the inside of your wrist. Your pulse tells you how fast your heart is beating. When you exercise, you need more oxygen, so you breathe faster. The heart beats faster to pump your blood, and the oxygen it carries, around the body.

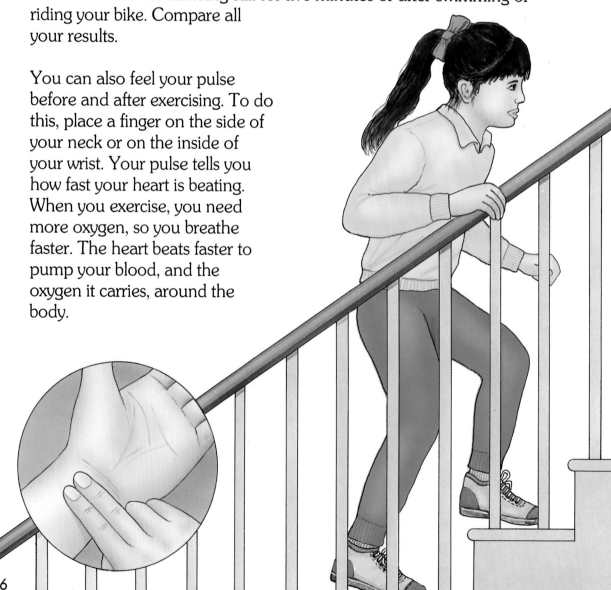

How Big Are Your Lungs?

This experiment will show the amount of air your lungs hold.

You will need:
a long piece of plastic tubing, masking tape, a large bottle which holds about a gallon of water, a waterproof pen, a measuring cup.

1. Fill a bathtub half full of water.
2. Fill the large bottle with water. Stick tape on one side.
3. Hold the bottle over the tub, cover the mouth with your hand, and carefully turn the bottle upside down. Keep your hand over the mouth; place bottle under water. Remove your hand. Ask a friend to mark the water level on the tape.
4. Push one end of the plastic tubing into the neck of the bottle.
5. Take a deep breath and blow as hard as you can down the tubing.
6. Mark the level of the water in the bottle when you have finished.
7. Cover the mouth with your hand and remove bottle from water. Turn it right side up. Use the measuring cup to pour water into the bottle up to the first mark you made on the side. The amount of water you add is roughly the same as the amount of air in your lungs. It is called your lung capacity.
8. Repeat the test after taking an ordinary breath. How much air do you breathe out this time? Compare your lung capacity with your friends'.

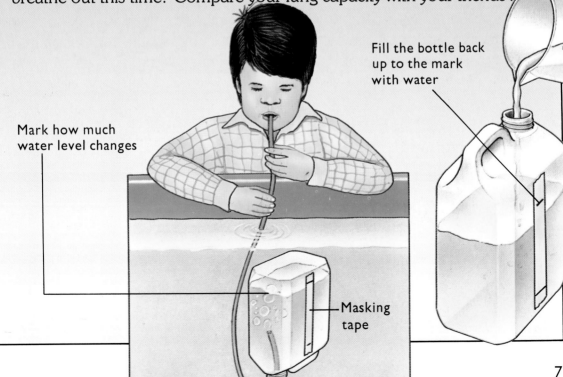

Fill the bottle back up to the mark with water

Mark how much water level changes

Masking tape

Candles and Burning

Things need oxygen in order to burn. Prove this with candles.

Fix two small candles firmly to saucers with modeling clay. Ask an adult to light the candles and put a small jar over one of them. How long does each burn?

What happens
The candle under the jar soon goes out because it uses up all the oxygen. The other candle has lots of oxygen around it, so it burns for a longer time. Try this test with a larger jar. How long does the candle burn this time?

▼ Have you ever noticed flaky brown or red patches on old cars? When iron is left in damp air, it joins with oxygen in the air to form a red powder which we call rust. Without oxygen, iron will not rust.

Make a Fruit Salad

You will need:
half a lemon, a lemon squeezer, a bowl, a saucer, a chopping board and knife, a spoon, fresh fruit, plastic wrap.

1. Squeeze the juice from the lemon and pour it into the bowl.
2. Ask an adult to help you slice up the fruit.
3. Put pieces of each fruit in the saucer and the rest in the bowl.
4. Spoon lemon juice over the fruit in the bowl.
5. Cover the bowl with plastic wrap and leave the saucer of fruit uncovered. Put both in the refrigerator. Which fruit goes brown?

What happens

The oxygen in the air reacts with the fruit, and chemical changes make the fruit in the saucer change color. But acid in the lemon juice helps to stop this chemical change from happening to the fruit in the bowl.

 Moldy Food

Floating in the air are the tiny spores of a group of fungi called molds. If these spores land on food, they start to feed and produce more spores. This makes the food turn moldy.

Leave some boiled potato, orange peel, cheese, and stale bread in old saucers on a windowsill. Sprinkle each with water. Which food gets moldy first? What color is the mold?

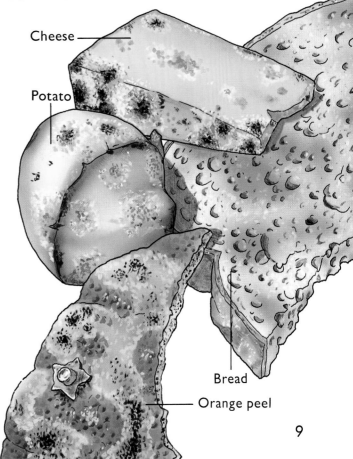

Cheese

Potato

Bread

Orange peel

You will need:
a small jar, a spoon, a tall bottle, sugar cubes, yeast (fresh or dried), a balloon, string.

Bubbles in Bread

Use the carbon dioxide given off by yeast to blow up a balloon.

1. Half fill a small jar with warm water and add four sugar cubes.
2. Use the spoon to stir the water until the sugar dissolves.
3. Pour the sugary water into the tall bottle.
4. Mix one teaspoon of the yeast with a little water.
5. Add this mixture to the bottle.
6. Use the string to tie the balloon over the neck of the bottle. Leave the bottle in a warm place.

Tie the balloon onto the top

Mixture

Yeast

Sugar

What happens
The yeast feeds on the sugar, grows, and gives off carbon dioxide gas. This gas will blow up the balloon. It also makes air holes in bread.

Making Cakes
If you make a cake with plain flour, you need to add baking powder to make the cake light and full of air. Baking powder, like yeast, gives off bubbles of carbon dioxide gas if mixed with water and heated.

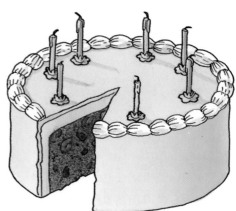

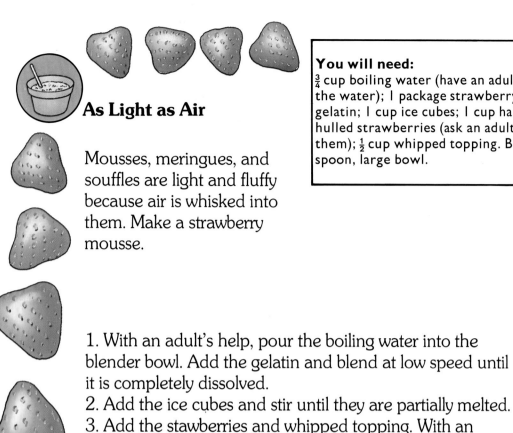

As Light as Air

Mousses, meringues, and souffles are light and fluffy because air is whisked into them. Make a strawberry mousse.

You will need:
$\frac{3}{4}$ cup boiling water (have an adult boil the water); 1 package strawberry gelatin; 1 cup ice cubes; 1 cup halved, hulled strawberries (ask an adult to cut them); $\frac{1}{2}$ cup whipped topping. Blender, spoon, large bowl.

1. With an adult's help, pour the boiling water into the blender bowl. Add the gelatin and blend at low speed until it is completely dissolved.
2. Add the ice cubes and stir until they are partially melted.
3. Add the stawberries and whipped topping. With an adult's help, blend at high speed for 30 seconds or until the mixture is smooth.
4. Pour the mixture into a large bowl and leave it in the refrigerator until it is firm (at least 30 minutes). When you eat the mousse, you will see lots of tiny bubbles of air.

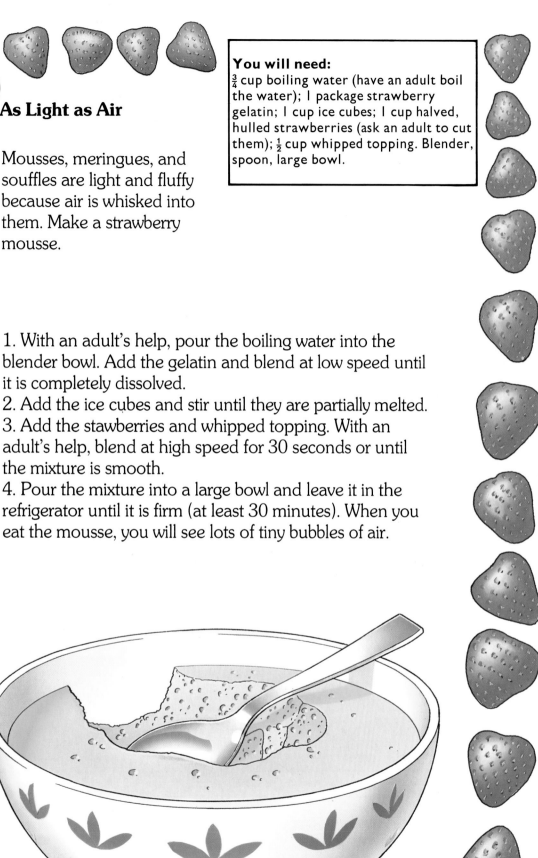

Have you ever watched an open-air fire? Sparks from the fire are carried upward by warm air rising from the fire. As air gets warmer, the particles of which it is made spread out. This makes the air lighter, or less dense, so it rises upward. As air cools, it becomes heavier, or more dense, and sinks downward again. When heat is carried by the air itself, the process is called convection.

Falling feathers

Let a small feather fall in different places around a room. Can you find any places where the feather will rise? (A warm radiator is a good place to try.) How high does the feather rise? How long is it in the air?

Bubbles will also help you to detect rising hot-air currents.

▲ Air inside a hot-air balloon is heated by a gas flame below the balloon. The hot air inside the balloon is lighter, or less dense, than the cooler air outside the balloon. As the hot air rises, it carries the balloon upward. When the gas flame is turned down, the air cools and the balloon sinks back to the ground.

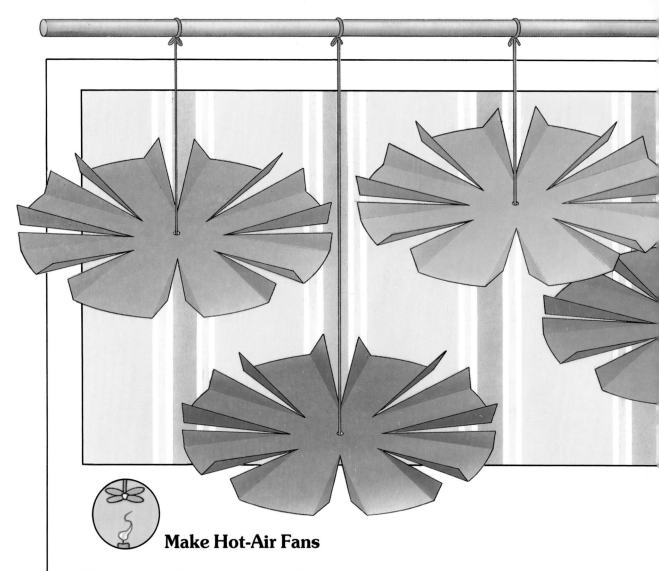

Make Hot-Air Fans

These fans will twirl around in rising currents of warm air.

You will need:
colored paper, a jar, a pencil, a ruler, scissors, thread, tape, a thin stick or piece of dowel.

1. On the colored paper, draw several circles by tracing around the outside of the jar. Make each circle about 4 inches across.
2. Cut out the circles.
3. Fold each circle in half, then in half again, and in half a third time.
4. Open out the circles. You should have eight fold lines in each circle.
5. On each fold line, measure $1\frac{1}{2}$ inches from the edge and put a pencil mark.
6. Cut along each fold line up to the pencil dot.
7. Bend up the cut edges so that each bends the same way.

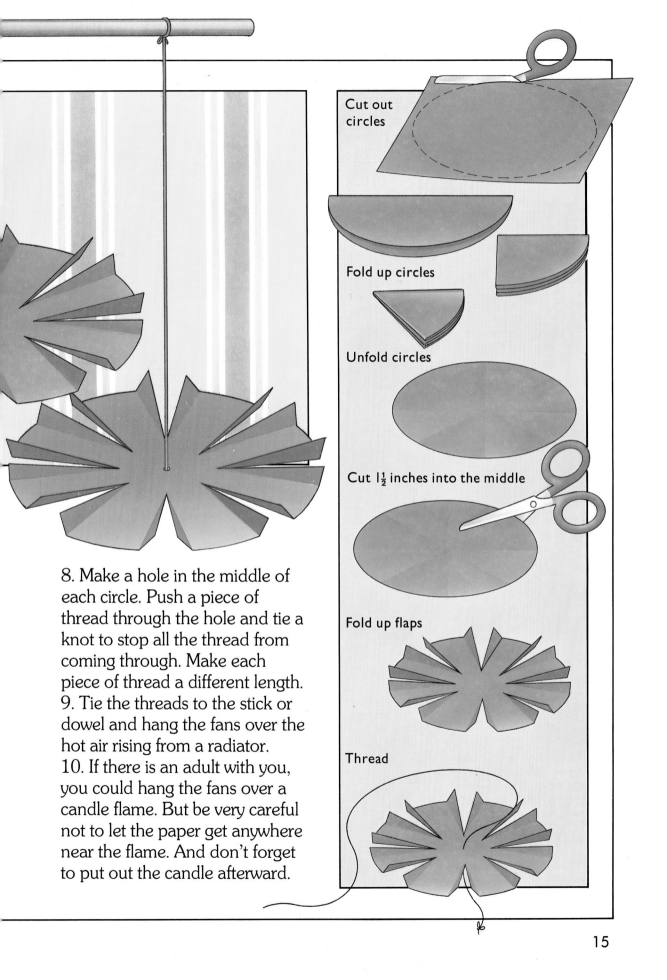

Cut out circles

Fold up circles

Unfold circles

Cut 1½ inches into the middle

Fold up flaps

Thread

8. Make a hole in the middle of each circle. Push a piece of thread through the hole and tie a knot to stop all the thread from coming through. Make each piece of thread a different length.

9. Tie the threads to the stick or dowel and hang the fans over the hot air rising from a radiator.

10. If there is an adult with you, you could hang the fans over a candle flame. But be very careful not to let the paper get anywhere near the flame. And don't forget to put out the candle afterward.

AIR PUSHES BACK

Can you use a balloon to lift up a plastic beaker? Put the balloon inside the beaker and blow up the balloon. You will find that the sides of the balloon grip the beaker tightly. You should be able to lift up the beaker just by holding on to the neck of the balloon.

This works because air can be squeezed or compressed into a smaller space. The compressed air inside the balloon presses outward on the sides of the beaker, so you can lift it up. Air pressure can be a powerful force.

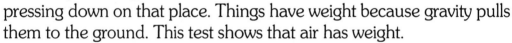

The air around us presses against us equally in all directions. The pressure of the air in any place is caused by the weight of all the air pressing down on that place. Things have weight because gravity pulls them to the ground. This test shows that air has weight.

Tie a piece of string to the middle of a thin stick and hang the string from a hook. Blow up two identical balloons, making one bigger than the other. Tie one balloon onto each end of the stick. The end with the bigger balloon will dip down. Because it contains more air, it is heavier than the smaller balloon.

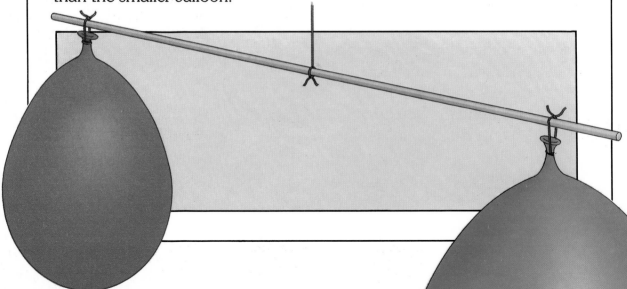

Upside-down Water

Hold a glass over a sink or a bowl and fill it right to the top with water. Carefully slide a smooth piece of cardboard, such as a postcard, over the top. Hold your hand on the card and slowly turn the glass upside down. When you take away your hand, what happens?

What happens
The air pushes against the card and should keep the water in the glass. The pressure of the air upward is greater than the pressure of the water downward.

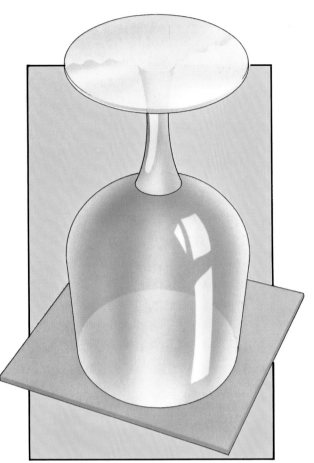

Make a Siphon

1. Fill two jars with water. Hold a plastic tube under water in a bowl until the air has escaped from it.
2. Pinch both tube ends and put one end under water in each jar. Lift one jar up and down.

What happens
When one jar is lower than the other, the air pressing down on the water in the top jar will force the water up the tube, and down into the other jar.

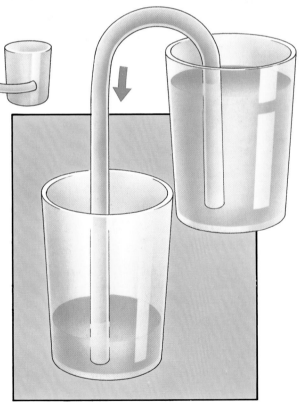

Make a Balloon Rocket

You will need:
a balloon, a straw, strong tape, scissors, strong thread.

1. Cut a straw in half and push one end of a long piece of thread through the straw.
2. Stretch the thread across a room and tie it tightly.
3. Cut two pieces of tape.
4. Blow a little air into the balloon.
5. Hold the end of the balloon tightly so the air cannot escape and ask a friend to help you tape the balloon firmly to the straw.
6. Blow some more air into the balloon.

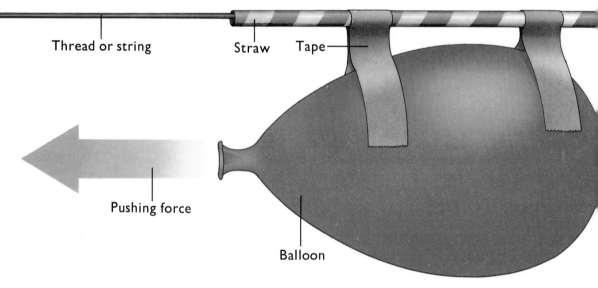

Thread or string   Straw   Tape

Pushing force

Balloon

7. When you let the balloon go, how fast does it travel? Can you think of a way of slowing down the rocket?
8. If you set up two balloon rockets side by side, you could have a race!

What happens
The air inside the balloon is squashed into a small space so it is at a high pressure. As it rushes out of the neck of the balloon, it pushes the balloon in the opposite direction. (The hot gases rushing out of the back of a jet airplane push it forward.)

▲ Powerful fans on an air-cushion
vehicle blow air under the craft,
which increases the air pressure
there. This higher pressure pushes
the craft off the ground or water so
it floats on a cushion of compressed
air. Propellers on the top of the
craft spin around to push the air
aside and drive the craft backward
or forward.

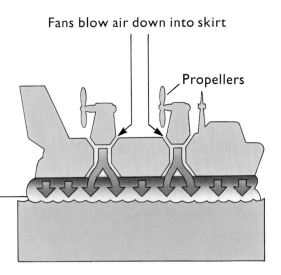

Fans blow air down into skirt

Propellers

Cushion of compressed air

Weather is produced by air moving from place to place—which we call winds. Winds are caused by warm air rising and cooler air moving in to take its place. Warm air is lighter, or less dense, than cool air, so it creates low air pressure. Cool air is heavier, or more dense, and creates high air pressure. Usually we have fine weather when the air pressure is high. Low air pressure brings clouds, rain, or snow.

▼ Winds can sometimes blow at tremendous speeds and cause great damage. The winds produced by a hurricane can travel at 80 to 100 miles an hour. This picture shows the damage from a hurricane in Darwin, Australia.

Make a Barometer

A barometer measures air pressure. A change in the air pressure tells us when the weather is likely to change.

You will need:
a tall, clear bottle, a bowl, two thin pieces of wood, tape, a pen.

1. Fill the bottle with water. Hold the bowl over the top of the bottle and carefully turn the bottle upside down. Some of the water will spill out, so do this over a sink or a bathtub.

2. Stand the bowl with the bottle inside it in a cool place.

3. Tilt the bottle to let some water out and some air in. It needs to be about one-third full of air.

4. Slip the pieces of wood under the bottle to lift it clear of the bowl. This lets water move in and out of the bottle.

5. Stick a long piece of tape on the side of the bottle and mark the level of the water.

6. Watch your barometer carefully and mark the level of the water at regular intervals. Can you predict the weather with your barometer?

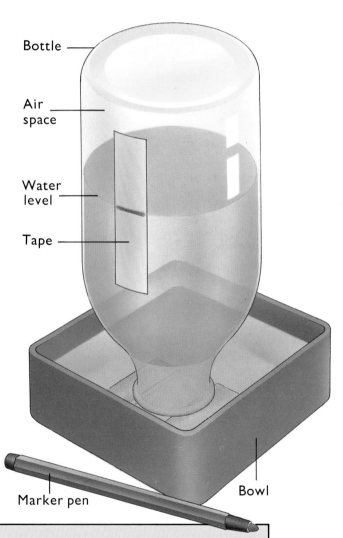

Bottle

Air space

Water level

Tape

Marker pen

Bowl

What happens
When the air pressure increases, it pushes down on the water in the bowl, forcing the water up the bottle. When the air pressure falls, the level of water in the bottle falls too. Better weather will usually follow when the barometer rises, and worse weather will follow when it falls.

Make a Wind Sock

A wind sock at an airport shows the strength and direction of the wind and helps pilots take off and land safely. Make a wind sock yourself.

1. With an adult's help, cut the shirt sleeve in half.
2. Bend the wire into a circle. Sew one end of the sleeve to the wire.
3. Tie string to the wire circle.
4. Tie the string to a long pole, such as an old broom handle.
5. Put your wind sock outside.

You will need:
an old shirt sleeve or stocking, scissors, wire, string, a nail, a pole or long stick.

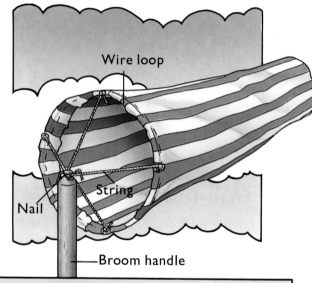

Wire loop

String

Nail

Broom handle

Measuring Wind Speed

You will need:
a cardboard box, dowel, a pen, cardboard, tape.

1. With an adult's help, cut off both ends of the box.
2. Draw a scale at one end.
3. Make a cardboard flap which will fit inside one end of the box.
4. Push the dowel through the sides of the box and stick the flap to the dowel. Make sure the flap of cardboard can swing freely.
5. Stick an arrow onto the dowel and put the wind speed measurer outside facing into the wind. How much does the flap move?

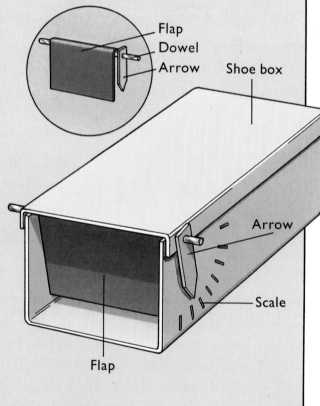

Flap
Dowel
Arrow
Shoe box

Arrow

Scale

Flap

Make a Windmill

1. Ask an adult to help you cut two short lengths of the half-inch square wood and drill a hole through the center point of each piece of wood.
2. Cut two small circles of cardboard and make a hole in the middle of each circle.
3. Push a thin piece of dowel through the hole in one piece of cardboard, through the holes in the wood, and out through the other cardboard circle. Glue the dowel to fix the wood in a cross shape.

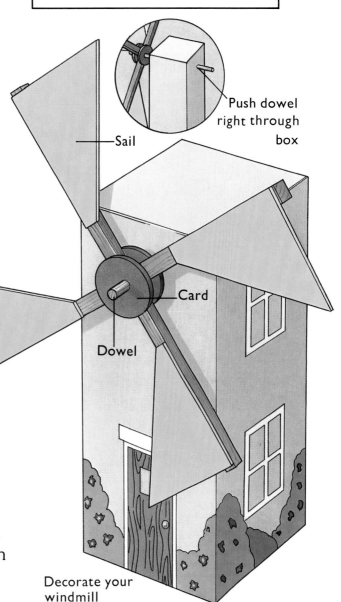

Push dowel right through box

Sail

Card

Dowel

Decorate your windmill

Wood

Sail

Push dowel through all holes and glue

4. Cut sails out of cardboard and fix them to the wooden cross with glue or tape.
5. Push the dowel through the side of the box near the top.
6. Put your windmill in a breeze outside or on a windowsill.
7. Can you use your windmill to lift something? Hint: fix a thread spool to the dowel at the back of the box.

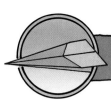 

How many flying things can you think of? Some flying things are alive. They are animals or parts of plants. Others are machines made by people.

You could make a scrapbook of flying things. Fill your scrapbook with drawings, postcards, and pictures cut out of newspapers or magazines.

Can you make a piece of paper fly through the air? First, drop the paper from a height. As the sheet of paper falls, air is trapped underneath. As the air escapes, it makes the paper sway.

Fold the paper in half and open it out. Fold one of the long edges back. Drop the paper from a height again.

The center fold makes the air pressure the same on both sides of the paper, and this keeps it from rolling from side to side. Folding a long edge makes one side of the paper heavier, so the paper pushes through air more easily.

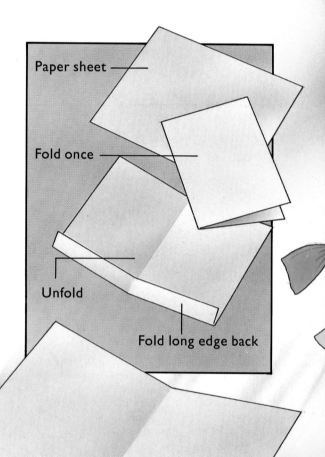

Paper sheet

Fold once

Unfold

Fold long edge back

▲ Have you ever seen people hang gliding? As the wings of the glider move through the air, they help to lift the glider upward. Warm air currents rising up from the ground also help to push the glider up into the sky.

Make a Flier

To find out more about how things move through the air, make a flier.

You will need:
thin balsa wood from a model store, rubber band, scissors, sandpaper, paints.

1. Use the scissors to cut two pieces of balsa wood about 1 inch wide by 6–8 inches long (ask an adult to help you). The size of the pieces is not that important, as long as they are both the same size.
2. Rub the sandpaper over the wood to make it smooth on both sides.
3. Hold the two pieces of wood in a cross shape and wrap the rubber band around them to fix them in this position.
4. Paint your flier any way you like.
5. Take your flier outside. Hold the tip of one piece of wood, lift the flier above your head, and throw it into a breeze. Try to spin it as you throw.

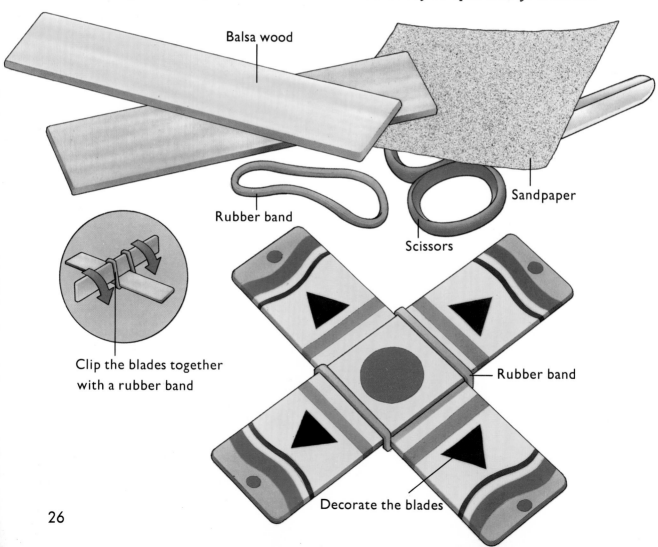

Balsa wood

Rubber band

Sandpaper

Scissors

Clip the blades together with a rubber band

Rubber band

Decorate the blades

How far does it fly? If you round off the corners of the wood, does it fly farther?

6. What happens if you fix the two pieces of wood so that one is standing up and the other lies flat?

▲ A gannet has a smooth, streamlined body shape, which helps it to fly fast through the air. You can find out more about birds and flight on pages 38–39.

What happens

As objects fly through the air, the air pulls against them and holds them back. This resistance to movement is called drag. Flying objects need enough energy to overcome drag and move through the air. By smoothing the wood with the sandpaper, you cut down the amount of drag. The flier with one piece of wood standing up creates a lot of air resistance and hardly flies at all. The flat flier creates less air resistance and flies much better.

Wings

Cut out a strip of paper about 8 inches long and 2 inches or more wide (ask an adult to help you). Fold the paper into a bridge shape and put the bridge on a flat surface. Blow steadily under the bridge. What happens to the bridge?

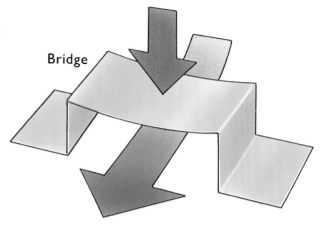

Bridge

Blow hard under the bridge

What happens

The top of the bridge moves down. When air moves fast, it is at a low pressure. Because the air pressure under the bridge is low, the higher air pressure on top pushes the bridge down. This link between air speed and air pressure is very important. It helps all sorts of flying things, from birds to airplanes, to fly.

Making Round Wings

1. Make a loop out of each strip of paper. Overlap the ends and tape them inside and outside the loop to match the picture.
2. Push the straw through the pockets in the loops and throw your plane horizontally.
3. How well does your straw plane fly? Try the loops in different positions along the straw. How does this affect the way the plane flies? Does the plane fly better with the small or the large loop in front?

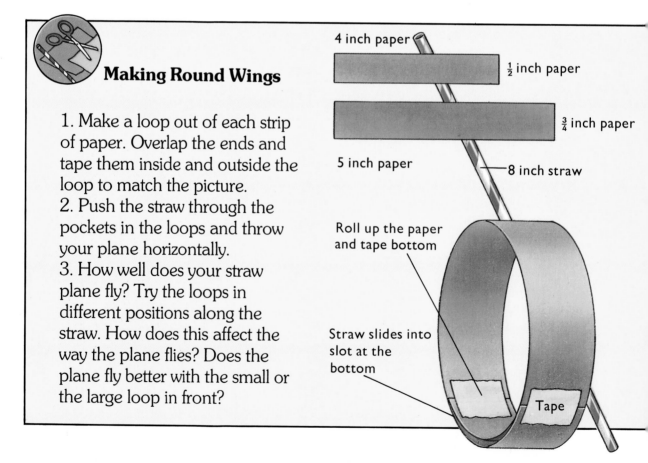

4 inch paper

$\frac{1}{2}$ inch paper

$\frac{3}{4}$ inch paper

5 inch paper

8 inch straw

Roll up the paper and tape bottom

Straw slides into slot at the bottom

Tape

Make a Wing

A wing is a special shape called an airfoil.

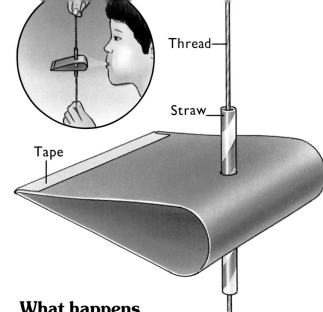

Thread

Straw

Tape

1. Cut a thin strip of paper about $1\frac{1}{2}$ inches wide and 10 inches long (ask an adult to help you).
2. Cut a short length of straw.
3. Bend and fold the paper into a wing shape.
4. Use tape to join the ends of the paper on top of the wing.
5. Push the straw through holes in the middle of the wing and fix it in place with tape.
6. Push a long piece of thread down through the straw.
7. Hold the thread and blow.

What happens

The air going over the top of the wing moves faster, and faster air means lower pressure. The slower air under the wing is at a higher pressure and pushes the wing up the thread. This upward pushing force is called lift.

What happens

The round wings on this plane work in the same way as flatter wings. The air moves more slowly under the wing and the higher air pressure lifts the plane up into the air.

Make Paper Gliders

Use paper about 12 inches by 8 inches. You can make paper gliders from different kinds of paper, such as newspaper, glossy magazine paper, crepe paper, or tissue paper. What is the best kind of material for making paper gliders?

1. Fold the paper in half down the middle of the long side and open it out again.
2. Fold the top corners over so they meet in the middle.
3. Fold the same corners to the middle once more.
4. Turn the paper over.
5. Fold the sides to the middle and then fold the glider in half.
6. Grip the glider firmly by the center fold and pull the wings flat.
7. Use tape to hold the wings together in the middle.
8. Add one or more paper clips or a small piece of modeling clay to the nose of the glider. Does the glider fly better?
9. Cut some small flaps in the end of the wings. Bend the flaps up and down and see how this changes the direction the glider flies in. See pages 32–33.

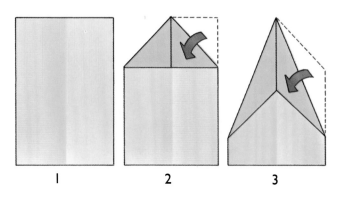

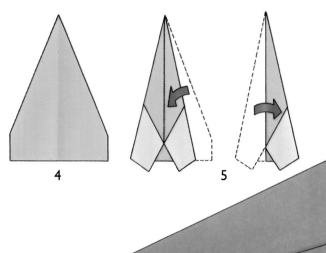

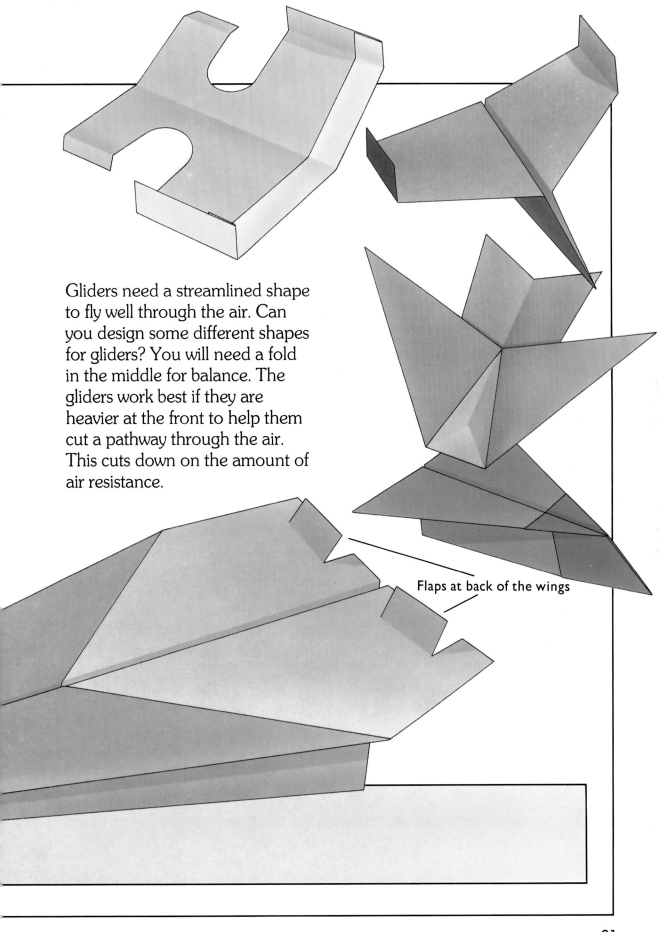

Gliders need a streamlined shape to fly well through the air. Can you design some different shapes for gliders? You will need a fold in the middle for balance. The gliders work best if they are heavier at the front to help them cut a pathway through the air. This cuts down on the amount of air resistance.

Flaps at back of the wings

▲ To take off, a plane uses its engines to move fast along the runway. As it moves, air flows above and below the wings and produces lift. When there is enough lift to overcome the force of gravity, the plane takes off. In the air, the plane is slowed down by the resistance, or drag, of the air. The power of the engines has to overcome this dragging effect to keep the plane moving.

 **Making an Airplane**

You will need:
a straw, paper clips, stiff paper, a pencil, tape, scissors.

1. Make a wing shape, with the top edge curved, from a piece of stiff paper about 10 inches by 5 inches.
2. Tape the back edge of the wing and cut ailerons in this edge (ask an adult to help you).
3. For the tail, cut a piece of stiff paper about 8 inches by $1\frac{1}{2}$ inches, and fold the middle so it sticks up. Cut away about $\frac{1}{3}$ inch of the flat pieces on either side of the tail.
4. Cut elevators in the flat edges of the tailpiece.
5. Use tape to fix the wings and tailpiece to the straw.
6. Weight the nose of the plane with several paper clips.

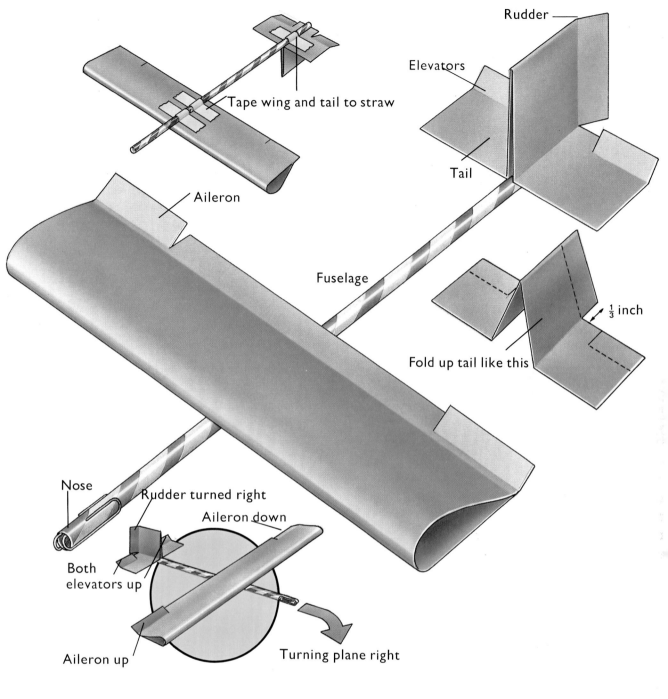

Rudder

Elevators

Tape wing and tail to straw

Tail

Aileron

Fuselage

$\frac{1}{3}$ inch

Fold up tail like this

Nose

Rudder turned right

Aileron down

Both elevators up

Aileron up

Turning plane right

7. Now bend the flaps up and down and the rudder from side to side to see how this affects the flight of the plane.

Have you ever noticed the flaps on the wings and tailpiece of a passenger airplane? The flaps on the wings are called ailerons. The ones on the tail piece are called elevators. The pilot moves the ailerons and elevators, together with a tail flap called the rudder, to make the plane turn, climb, or dive through the air. Make your own airplane, and see how this works.

Spinning Around

Have you ever watched a maple seed falling off a tree? As it spins around and around, the air rushing above and below the wing shape produces lift. This helps the seed to fly away from the parent tree. If it lands too near the parent, it is not likely to find enough space, light, and water to grow into a new tree.

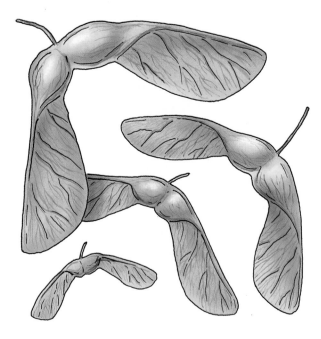

▼ Each one of the long, thin rotor blades on top of a helicopter is like the "wing" of a maple seed. It is a long, narrow airfoil. A helicopter stands still and turns its rotors to make air rush past its "wings." The faster the rotors spin, the faster the air moves and the more lift is produced.

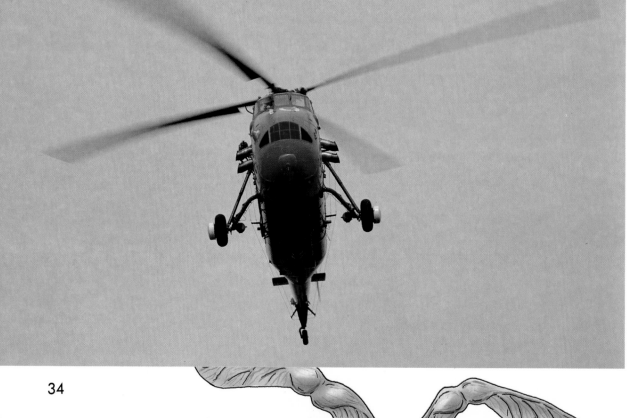

Make a Paper Helicopter

1. On paper about 8 inches by $2\frac{1}{2}$ inches, draw a shape like the picture and cut it out.*
2. Cut along the center line.*
3. Fold along the dotted line so that one rotor bends forward and the other backward.
4. Push a paper clip onto the other end of the paper.
5. Drop your helicopter from a height and watch how it spins.
6. Bend the rotors the other way. In which direction does the helicopter spin now?
7. Drop your helicopter upside down. Will it turn the right way up again?

*Ask an adult to help you.

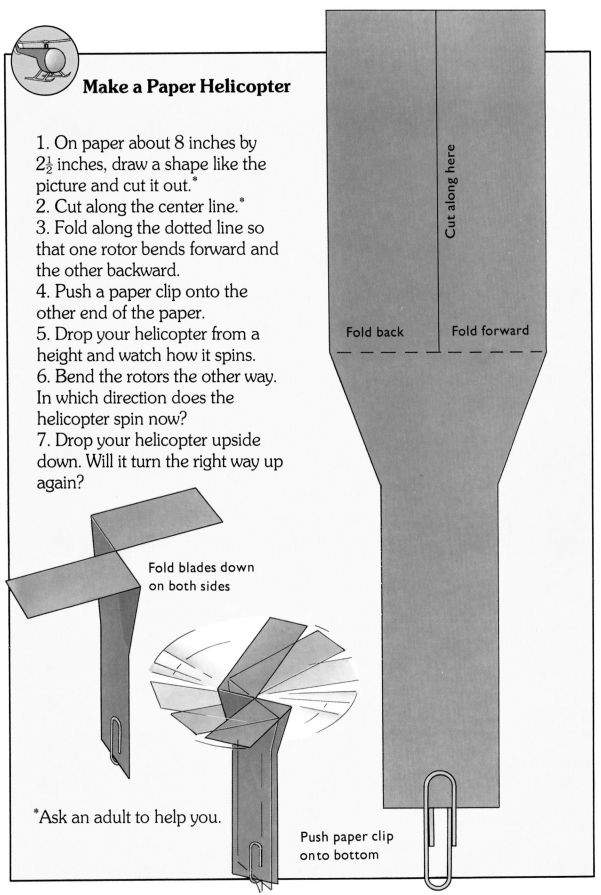

Cut along here

Fold back

Fold forward

Fold blades down on both sides

Push paper clip onto bottom

 Drifting Through the Air

Air resistance can sometimes be useful if we want to slow flying things down. For instance, parachutes slow down things falling to the ground. A dandelion seed has a little parachute to help it drift slowly on the wind. This helps it to cover long distances and to move away from its parent plant.

Make Parachutes

You will need:
scissors, thread or string, different fabrics, and loads.

1. With an adult's help, cut different-sized squares out of the fabrics.
2. Use tape to fix thread or string to each corner of the squares.
3. Tie a load to the strings under each parachute, and launch it.
4. How long does each parachute take to fall down to the ground? Do larger parachutes fall more quickly or more slowly? Does it make a difference if the parachute is carrying a heavy load?
5. Make a small hole in the top of one of the parachutes. How does this affect the way it falls?

What happens
The force of gravity pulls the parachute down to the ground. But some air is trapped under the parachute. This air gets squashed and pushes up against the parachute, making the parachute fall more slowly.

▲ Modern parachutes have a hole in the top. This helps the air trapped inside the parachute escape more smoothly and stops the parachute from wobbling and swaying as it falls through the air.

▶ Some animals, such as the colugo (right), have flaps of skin along the sides of the body. When they spread this skin, they can glide through the air like living parachutes. The colugo can glide as far as 450 feet between trees.

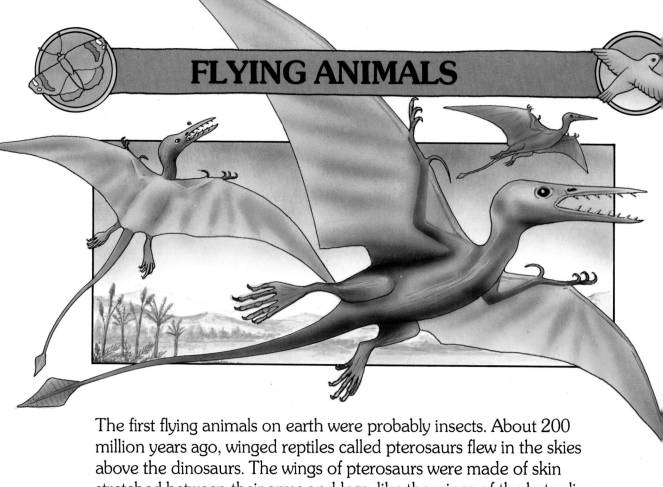

FLYING ANIMALS

The first flying animals on earth were probably insects. About 200 million years ago, winged reptiles called pterosaurs flew in the skies above the dinosaurs. The wings of pterosaurs were made of skin stretched between their arms and legs, like the wings of the bats alive today. The largest pterosaurs had wings that were as big as those of a small airplane.

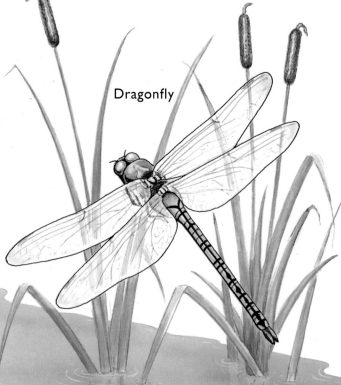

Dragonfly

Today, only birds, bats, and insects have wings to power flight upward instead of just gliding along. Being able to fly is very useful. It helps animals escape from danger as well as find food and places to nest.

Insects have very thin, flat wings with powerful muscles. As they flap their wings, they push against the air, and this makes them move upward and forward. Flies can beat their wings as fast as 1,000 times a second.

▲ As a bird's wings beat downward, they create more air pressure under the wings. This extra pressure pushes the bird upward. When the wings are pulled up again, the tips of the feathers move apart to let air flow through.

▼ Hummingbirds are like tiny helicopters. They can fly sideways, backward, and upside down. Hummingbirds beat their wings between 22 and 78 times a second and can fly up to 40 miles per hour.

Birds are well-designed living flying machines. Their bodies are light in weight, and some of their bones are hollow to reduce weight. Their feathers fit closely together to give them a smooth, streamlined shape. And their front arms have become wings. A bird's wing is shaped like an airfoil to give it lift. Birds have very powerful chest muscles to beat their wings up and down.

INDEX

Adviser: Robert Pressling
Designer: Robert Pressling
Editor: Catherine Bradley
Picture Research: Elaine Willis

The publishers wish to thank the following for kindly supplying photographs for this book:
Page 5 ZEFA; 8 J. Allan Cash; 13 ZEFA; 19 ZEFA; 20 Frank Lane Picture Agency; 25 Life Science Images; 27 Frank Lane Picture Agency; 32 Boeing; 34 Life Science Images; 37 Ministry of Defence; 39 Swift Picture Library.

First Random House edition, 1992

Library of Congress Cataloging-in-Publication Data

Taylor, Barbara, 1954–
  [Air and flight (Warwick Press)]
  Up, up & away!: the science of flight/Barbara Taylor.—1st Random House ed.
  p.—cm.—(Step into science)
  Reprint. Originally published: Air and flight. New York: Warwick Press, 1991. Originally published in series: Fun with simple science.
  Includes index.
  Summary: An introduction to the science of flight using simple experiments to show how animals and machines fly, how moving air causes weather, and more.
  ISBN: 0-679-82039-6 (pbk.)
  1. Air—Juvenile literature. 2. Air—Experiments——Juvenile literature. 3. Flight—Juvenile literature. 4. Flight—Experiments—Juvenile literature. [1. Air—Experiments. 2. Flight—Experiments. 3. Experiments.] I. Title. II. Title: Up, up & away! III. Series: Taylor, Barbara, 1954– Step into science.
  QC161.2.T4   1992
  533'.6'078—dc20   91-4292

Manufactured in Hong Kong 10 9 8 7 6 5 4 3 2 1